Ve

Cookbook

© Copyright 2018. Laura Sommers.
All rights reserved.
No part of this book may be reproduced in any form or by any electronic or mechanical means without written permission of the author. All text, illustrations and design are the exclusive property of
Laura Sommers

Introduction	1
Venison Stew	2
Slow Cooker Venison Stew	3
Sloppy Does	4
Venison Chili	5
Slow Cooker Apple-Scented Venison Roast	6
Venison Stroganoff	7
Venison Bacon Burgers	8
Breaded Venison	9
Venison And Red Currant Casserole	10
Barbecue Venison	11
Country Style Venison Steaks	12
Venison Fajitas	13
Venison Italian Soup	14
Venison Soup	15
Venison And Gravy	16
Fried Buck Nuggets	17
Venison Meatballs	18
Venison Applesauce Meatballs	19
Mongolian Venison Meatballs	20
Bacon-Wrapped Venison Meatballs	21
Middle Eastern Venison Meatballs	22
Waikiki Venison Meatballs	23

Mexican Venison Chili 24
Feta and Olive Venison Meatballs 25
Venison Stuffed Green Peppers 26
Venison Stroganoff 27
Mustard Fried Venison 28
Venison Gyros 29
Teriyaki Venison 30
Venison & Wild Rice Casserole 31
Venison & Wild Rice Stew 32
Sweet And Sour Venison Stew 33
Cajun Venison 34
Venison Goulash 35
Venison Hash 36
Venison Cider Stew 37
Venison Fingers 38
Venison Cream Cheese Casserole 39
Venison Jerky 40
Tabasco Venison Jerky 41
Venison Pizzas 42
Venison Sauerbraten 43
Venison Vegetable Pot Pie 44
Venison Shepherd's Pie 45
Venison Swedish Meatballs 46
Venison Summer Sausage 47

Venison Zucchini Lasagna 48

Venison-Stuffed Cabbage Leaves 49

Broccoli Venison Casserole 50

Venison Chili Con Carne 51

Chicken Fried Venison, Steak 52

Burgundy Venison 53

Cranberry Venison Stew 54

Venison Breakfast Sausage 55

Bacon-Wrapped Venison Tenderloin 56

Venison Pot Roast and Gravy 57

Venison-Bacon White Chili 58

Mexican Venison Skillet 59

Fried Venison Backstrap 60

Baked Spaghetti with Venison 61

Venison Wellington 62

Texas Venison 63

Venison Pastrami 64

Corned Venison 65

Venison with Blackberry Wine Sauce 66

Venison Tequila Chili 67

Venison Pasta Casserole 68

Spicy Venison Meatballs 69

Texas Venison Corn Chowder 70

Cheddar Venison Stuffed Peppers 71

About the Author 72
Other Books by Laura Sommers 73

Introduction

From the woods to the table, avid deer hunters love to be the star chef at every dinner and cookout. The Venison Cookbook will take you beyond chili and stew and introduces many delicious and delightful recipes using the fresh venison deer meat from the season's hunt.

This cookbook is full of mouth-watering and scrumptious meals for you to make for family and guests including casseroles, pies, steaks and jerky. Venison is a healthy and delicious ingredient for homesteaders, campers, hunters and outdoor enthusiasts.

Venison Stew

Ingredients:

2 tbsps. olive oil
1 onion, chopped
White Onion, Large
2 cloves minced garlic
1 pound venison, cut into strips
1 (28 oz.) can diced tomatoes
1 (8 oz.) can sliced mushrooms, drained
1/2 tsp. dried thyme
1/2 tsp. dried sage
1/4 tsp. dried tarragon
1/4 tsp. salt

Directions:

1. Heat the olive oil in a large skillet over medium heat; cook and stir the onion and garlic in the hot oil until the onion is translucent, about 5 minutes.
2. Add the venison to the skillet; cook and stir until evenly browned.
3. Stir the tomatoes, mushrooms, thyme, sage, tarragon, and salt into the mixture; cover the skillet and allow the mixture to simmer until the venison is tender, 30 to 40 minutes.

Slow Cooker Venison Stew

Ingredients:

3 stalks celery, diced
1/2 cup chopped onion
2 cloves garlic, minced
1 tbsp. chopped fresh parsley
2 tbsps. vegetable oil
2 pounds venison stew meat
Salt and pepper to taste
Dried oregano to taste
Dried basil to taste
1 cup tomato sauce
1/2 cup dry red wine
1/2 cup water

Directions:

1. Place the celery, onion, garlic, and parsley in the bottom of a slow cooker.
2. Heat the oil in a large frying pan over medium-high heat.
3. Brown the venison well in two batches, and add to the slow cooker.
4. Season to taste with salt, pepper, oregano, and basil.
5. Pour in the tomato sauce, red wine, and water.
6. Cook on Low for 7 to 10 hours.

Sloppy Does

Ingredients:

1 tsp. olive oil
1 pound ground venison
1 jalapeno pepper, seeded and diced
1/2 cup ketchup
1 clove garlic, diced
2 tsps. molasses
1 tsp. prepared yellow mustard

Directions:

1. Heat olive oil in a skillet over medium heat; brown ground venison with jalapeno pepper in the hot oil, stirring often, until meat is crumbly and no longer pink, about 10 minutes.
2. Stir ketchup, garlic, molasses, and yellow mustard into the venison mixture, bring to a boil, and reduce heat to low. Simmer at least 10 minutes.

Venison Chili

Ingredients:

4 tbsps. unsalted butter
1 red onion, chopped
4 cloves garlic, minced
4 tbsps. dark brown sugar
3 cups red wine
4 tbsps. red wine vinegar
4 tbsps. tomato paste
4 cups low-sodium chicken broth
1 tsp. ground cumin
1/2 tsp. cayenne pepper
1/2 tsp. chili powder
2 tbsps. chopped fresh cilantro
Salt to taste4 tbsps. canola oil
10 slices cooked bacon, diced
2 pounds venison stew meat, diced
2 cups black beans, cooked and drained

Directions:

1. Melt the butter in a large pot over medium heat.
2. Stir in the onion and garlic, and sauté for 3 to 4 minutes.
3. Stir in the brown sugar and sauté for 2 to 3 more minutes.
4. Then stir in the red wine, vinegar, tomato paste, chicken stock, cumin, cayenne pepper, chili powder, cilantro and salt. Simmer for 30 to 35 minutes, or until the mixture is reduced by about half.
5. Meanwhile, heat the oil in a large skillet over medium-high heat.
6. Stir in the bacon and fry for 3 to 4 minutes, or until the bacon is browned. Move the bacon to one side of the skillet and add the venison to the empty side of the skillet.
7. Season the meat with salt to taste and sauté the meat for 15 minutes, or until well browned.
8. Stir in the beans and toss all together. Transfer this mixture to the simmering pot.
9. Mix everything together thoroughly and let simmer for about 20 more minutes.

Slow Cooker Apple-Scented Venison Roast

Ingredients:

1 tbsp. olive oil
3 pounds boneless venison roast
1 large apple, cored and quartered
2 small onions, sliced
4 cloves crushed garlic
1 cup boiling water
1 cube beef bouillon

Directions:

1. Spread the olive oil on the inside of a slow cooker.
2. Place the venison roast inside, and cover with apple, onions, and garlic.
3. Turn to Low, and cook until the roast is tender, about 6 to 8 hours.
4. When the roast has cooked, remove it from the slow cooker, and place onto a serving platter. Discard the apple.
5. Stir the water and bouillon into the slow cooker until the bouillon has dissolved.
6. Serve this as a sauce with the roast.

Venison Stroganoff

Ingredients:

1 pound venison, cut into cubes
Salt and pepper to taste
garlic powder to taste
1 onion, chopped
2 (10.75 oz.) cans condensed cream of mushroom soup
1 (16 oz.) package uncooked egg noodles
1 (8 oz.) container sour cream

Directions:

1. Season venison with salt, pepper and garlic powder to taste.
2. Sauté onion in a large skillet; when soft, add venison and brown.
3. Drain when venison is no longer pink and add soup.
4. Reduce heat to low and simmer.
5. Meanwhile, bring a large pot of lightly salted water to a boil.
6. Add noodles and cook for 8 to 10 minutes or until al dente; drain.
7. When noodles are almost done cooking, stir sour cream into meat mixture.
8. Pour meat mixture over hot cooked noodles and serve.

Venison Bacon Burgers

Ingredients:

1 pound peppercorn bacon, diced
5 pounds ground venison
2 cups bread crumbs
1/2 cup Worcestershire sauce
1/4 cup evaporated milk
5 cloves garlic, minced
1 tsp. ground cayenne pepper

Directions:

1. Preheat an outdoor grill for medium-high heat and lightly oil the grate.
2. Place bacon in a stainless steel bowl; add venison, bread crumbs, Worcestershire sauce, milk, garlic, and cayenne pepper.
3. Mix venison mixture using your hands and form into 5-oz. balls. Press balls with the back of a side dish to form patties.
4. Grill patties on the preheated grill until desired doneness is reached, about 5 minutes per side. An instant-read thermometer inserted into the center should read at least 160 degrees F (70 degrees C).

Breaded Venison

Ingredients:

2 lbs. venison, cut into 1/4 inch slices
1 cup fresh lemon juice
Salt
Freshly ground black pepper
2 eggs
1/4 cup flour
garlic and onion powder
2 tbsp. water
1 cup fine bread crumbs
1 1/2 cup shortening or vegetable oil

Directions:

1. In a glass baking dish, marinate the cutlets in lemon juice for 1 hour. Pat them dry with paper towels and sprinkle with salt and pepper.
2. Combine flour, bread crumbs, 1/4 tsp each of: salt, pepper, garlic and onion powder.
3. Dip cutlets into eggs beaten with water; then press them into the flour mixture, shaking off any excess. Refrigerate for at least 30 minutes.
4. Heat shortening or oil in a heavy 12-inch skillet until hot then add cutlets.
5. Cook over medium heat for 3-4 minutes on each side or until golden brown and cooked through.
6. Thicker portions require a longer cooking time and lower heat; thinner cutlets cook more quickly and at a higher temperature for good browning.
7. Use tongs to turn the cutlets in the oil once. Lift from oil using a slotted spoon and drain on brown paper or paper towels.
8. Season to taste with salt and pepper or other seasonings while still hot (we like Tony Cacheries and garlic powder).
9. Garnish with lemon wedges and serve immediately.

Venison And Red Currant Casserole

Ingredients:

3/4 lb diced venison
1/3 lb diced braising steak
1 large onion, chopped roughly
6 medium field mushrooms, thickly sliced
1 level tbsp. plain flour
2 oz. red currants
1-2 tbsps. red currant jelly
2 sprigs fresh thyme, or 1/2 tsp. dried
1 can fresh stock (beef or chicken)
1/2 pint red wine

Directions:

1. This casserole is best cooked in a cast-iron casserole dish, which will transfer from stovetop to oven.
2. Heat some olive oil and seal the meat over a medium heat.
3. Add onions and sweat for about 5 minutes.
4. Add mushrooms and thyme and cook for another couple of minutes.
5. Add red currants, stock red currant jelly, and wine.
6. Bring to the boil and then return the meat.
7. Cover the casserole and cook for 1 hour 45 minutes.
8. Remove lid and check how tender the meat is.
9. Continue to cook until finished up to one hour more.
10. Serve and enjoy!

Barbecue Venison

Ingredients:

3 to 4 lb. venison, well trimmed
3 tbsp. bacon drippings
1 onion, sliced
2 tbsp. green pepper
1 cup catsup
1 1/2 tsp. salt
1 1/2 tsp. celery seed
3 tbsp. brown sugar
3 tbsp. lemon juice
2 1/2 tsp. dry mustard
1/2 - to 3/4 cup water

Directions:

1. Brown venison in bacon drippings.
2. Pour off fat.
3. Mix remaining ingredients together and pour over meat in crockpot.
4. Cook 10 to 12 hours on low. Thicken sauce with 2 tbsps. cornstarch in 1/4 cup cold water. Shred meat on plate with 2 forks.
5. If returned to crockpot for 10 to 15 more minutes it absorbs more of the sauce.

Country Style Venison Steaks

Ingredients:

6 venison steaks, cut 1/2" to 5/8" thick
Salt & pepper
Charcoal seasoning
Butter

Directions:

1. One hour before broiling sprinkle both sides of steak generously and salt and pepper and add charcoal seasoning.
2. Preheat skillet.
3. Melt butter.
4. Pan broil steaks on medium high heat for 3 to 5 minutes per side.
5. Fry steaks separately or 2 at a time, using plenty of butter as venison is a lean meat.
6. Serve and enjoy!

Venison Fajitas

Fajita Seasoning Ingredients:

2 tsps. seasoned salt
1/4 tsp. garlic salt
1/2 tsp. black pepper
1/2 tsp. cayenne pepper
1 tsp. dried oregano
1 1/2 pounds venison, cut into 2 inch strips
4 tbsps. vegetable oil
1 medium red bell pepper, cut into 2 inch strips
1 medium yellow bell pepper, cut into 2 inch strips
1 medium onion, cut into 1/2-inch wedges
12 fajita size flour tortillas, warmed

Directions:

1. Combine seasoned salt, garlic salt, black pepper, cayenne pepper, and oregano to make the fajita seasoning.
2. Sprinkle two tsps. of the seasoning over the sliced venison.
3. Mix well, cover, and refrigerate for 30 minutes.
4. Heat 2 tbsps. of oil in a heavy frying pan.
5. Cook bell peppers and onion until starting to soften, then remove.
6. Pour in remaining oil, then cook venison until browned.
7. Return pepper mixture to the pan, season with remaining fajita seasoning, and reheat.
8. Served with the warmed tortillas.

Venison Italian Soup

Ingredients:

1 pound ground venison1 onion, chopped
1 (14.5 oz.) can stewed tomatoes
2 (8 oz.) cans tomato sauce
3 cups water
1 tbsp. minced garlic
2 tsps. dried basil
2 tsps. dried oregano
1 tsp. salt
1/2 tsp. ground black pepper
1 (15 oz.) can pinto beans
1 (15 oz.) can green beans
1 carrot, chopped
1 zucchini, chopped
1/2 (16 oz.) package fusilli (spiral) pasta

Directions:

1. Brown venison, onion, and garlic over medium heat until meat is no longer pink.
2. Add tomatoes, tomato sauce, water, and spices.
3. Bring to a boil, and then simmer for about 30 minutes.
4. Stir in beans, carrots, and zucchini. Simmer soup for 90 minutes.
5. Add pasta, and cook until tender.
6. Top individual servings with grated cheese, and serve.

Venison Soup

Ingredients:

1 lb. diced venison, cut into 1/2 inch cubes
Milk (for marinade)
1 (16 oz.) pkg. frozen mixed vegetables
6 green onions
1 (16 oz.) can tomatoes
1/2 tsp. salt
1/4 to 1/2 tsp. pepper
2 cup water or venison stock

Directions:

1. Using a glass container, soak the venison in milk for 12 hours or overnight. When you are ready to cook, drain the meat and put it into a suitable pot with water or venison stock.
2. Chop the tomatoes and put them, along with the juice from the can, into the pot.
3. Bring to a boil, cover, reduce heat and simmer for an hour and a half. If your venison is very tender, you can cut back on cooking time.
4. Chop the onions, including about half of the green tops, and put them into the pot along with the frozen vegetables, salt and pepper.
5. Serve and enjoy!

Venison And Gravy

Ingredients:

6 med. pieces venison, sirloin cuts
1 cup flour
1/4 tsp. salt
1 dash pepper
1/4 lb. pork
Mashed potatoes for serving

Directions:

1. Pound venison until tender. Brown salt pork on both sides.
2. Coat pieces of venison with flour and brown on both sides in salt pork drippings.
3. When evenly browned add enough water to cover venison and let simmer 1/2 hour until venison is tender.
4. Mix 1/4 cup flour and water then add to ingredients, this makes very delicious gravy over mashed potatoes.

Fried Buck Nuggets

Ingredients:

2 lbs. venison steak
Salt and pepper to taste
1 cup flour
1 cup oil

Directions:

1. Cut venison steak into 1/2 inch strips.
2. Salt and pepper steak, place steak in a plastic bag with flour.
3. Shake and then fry in hot oil.
4. Serve with rice and gravy.

Venison Meatballs

Ingredients:

2 lbs. venison, ground
1 egg
1 cup oatmeal
1 tsp. creole seasoning
1 qt. tomatoes
1 sm. onion
1 bell pepper

Directions:

1. Mix venison, oatmeal, egg, creole seasoning.
2. Make in small balls.
3. Place in fry pan with a small amount of cooking oil, fry one side, carefully turn over.
4. Slice onion, lay on top, slice pepper also.
5. Empty tomatoes over meat. Let it simmer for 1 hour or until peppers and onions are done.
6. When it sets for a while it absorbs lot of the liquid.

Venison Applesauce Meatballs

Ingredients:

1 cup applesauce
1 egg
1 cup bread crumbs
1/2 tsp. salt and pepper to taste
1 pound ground venison
Flour
1 tbsp. vegetable oil
4 carrots, peeled and thinly sliced
2 onions, thinly sliced
3 cups tomato juice

Directions:

1. Preheat oven to 350 degrees F (175 degrees C).
2. Combine applesauce, egg, bread crumbs, and salt and pepper, with ground venison; mix until well blended.
3. Form mixture into medium-sized meatballs, and roll in flour.
4. Heat 1 tsp. of oil in a large skillet over medium high or high heat.
5. Cook meatballs, turning occasionally, until evenly browned but not cooked through.
6. Transfer to a baking dish and set aside.
7. In the same skillet, partially cook the carrots and onions over medium high heat.
8. Add tomato juice, season to taste with salt and pepper, and bring to a boil.
9. Reduce heat, and simmer for 5 minutes, then pour over meatballs.
10. Cook, covered, in the preheated oven for 45 minutes, or until carrots are tender and meatballs are cooked through.
11. Cook uncovered for 10 minutes before removing from the oven.

Mongolian Venison Meatballs

Mongolian Sauce Ingredients:

1/2 cup hoisin sauce
4 cloves garlic, minced
2 tbsps. red wine vinegar
1 1/2 tbsps. soy sauce
1 tbsp. grated fresh ginger
1 tbsp. rice vinegar
2 tsps. sesame oil
2 tsps. white sugar
1 1/2 tsps. hot sauce
1/2 tsp. ground white pepper
1/2 tsp. ground black pepper

Meatballs Ingredients:

1 pound ground venison
1/2 pound ground lamb
1/2 head cabbage, chopped
1 yellow onion, chopped
1/2 cup panko bread crumbs
1/2 cup grated carrot
1 tbsp. ground ginger
1/4 cup chopped green onion
6 cloves garlic, chopped
1 tsp. garlic salt
1/2 tsp. ground black pepper

Directions:

1. Preheat oven to 450 degrees F (230 degrees C).
2. Whisk hoisin sauce, 4 cloves garlic, red wine vinegar, soy sauce, grated ginger, rice vinegar, sesame oil, sugar, hot sauce, white pepper, and black pepper together in a large bowl.
3. Mix ground venison, ground lamb, cabbage, yellow onion, panko, carrot, ground ginger, green onion, 6 cloves chopped garlic, garlic salt, black pepper, and 2 tbsps. of the hoisin sauce mixture together in a separate bowl; shape into meatballs and arrange on a jelly roll pan.
4. Bake in preheated oven until no longer pink in the middle, about 25 minutes.
5. Shake pan to turn meatballs, switch oven to Broil, and cook under the broiler until browned, about 10 minutes more.
6. Set aside to cool.
7. Transfer warm meatballs to slow cooker and pour hoisin sauce mixture over the meatballs.
8. Cook on Low, stirring intermittently, for 2 to 4 hours.

Bacon-Wrapped Venison Meatballs

Ingredients:

3 pounds ground venison
3 eggs
1/2 cup grated Parmesan cheese
1/4 cup chopped fresh parsley
1/2 cup dry bread crumbs
1 tbsp. minced garlic
1 tbsp. onion powder
1 tsp. salt
1 tsp. ground black pepper
1 tsp. dried oregano
1 tsp. dried basil
1 pound sliced bacon, cut in half crosswise

Directions:

1. Preheat oven to 350 degrees F (175 degrees C).
2. Line a rimmed baking sheet with parchment paper.
3. Mix ground venison, eggs, Parmesan cheese, parsley, bread crumbs, garlic, onion powder, salt, black pepper, oregano, and basil in a large bowl until thoroughly combined.
4. Form meat mix into 2-inch meatballs.
5. Wrap half a bacon slice around a meatball; turn the meatball around 45 degrees and wrap a second half-slice of bacon around the meatball so the meat is enclosed by bacon.
6. Repeat, forming 12 meatballs and wrapping each one in 2 half-slices of bacon.
7. Place wrapped meatballs onto the prepared baking sheet with seam sides down.
8. Bake in the preheated oven until meatballs are no longer pink inside and bacon is crisp, about 45 minutes.
9. An instant-read meat thermometer inserted into the center of a meatball should read at least 160 degrees F (70 degrees C).
10. Pour off excess grease.
11. Serve and enjoy!

Middle Eastern Venison Meatballs

Meatball Ingredients:

1 1/2 pounds lean ground venison
1 egg
2 tbsps. minced garlic
1/4 cup bread crumbs
1/2 tsp. cumin
Salt and pepper to taste
3 tbsps. vegetable oil
Tomato Sauce:
1 1/2 cups water
3 tbsps. tomato paste
2 tbsps. lemon juice
1/4 tsp. garlic powder
Salt and pepper to taste

Directions:

1. Combine the ground venison, egg, garlic, bread crumbs, cumin, salt, and pepper in a large bowl until well mixed.
2. Roll the mixture into egg-sized balls, and set aside.
3. Heat the vegetable oil in a large skillet over medium-high heat.
4. Add the meatballs; cook until firm, and browned on all sides, about 10 minutes.
5. Remove meatballs from the skillet and pour out the fat.
6. Bring the water to a boil in the same skillet over medium-high heat.
7. Stir in the tomato paste, lemon juice, garlic powder, salt, and pepper.
8. Bring to a boil, then reduce heat to medium.
9. Add the cooked meatballs, and simmer in the tomato sauce for 5 to 10 minutes until completely cooked.

Waikiki Venison Meatballs

Ingredients:

1 1/2 pounds ground venison
2/3 cup crushed saltine cracker crumbs
1/3 cup minced onion
1 egg
1/4 cup milk
1 1/2 tsps. ground ginger
1/2 tsp. salt
1 tbsp. olive oil
2 tbsps. cornstarch
1/2 cup packed brown sugar
1 (15 oz.) can pineapple chunks, drained, with juice reserved
1/3 cup white vinegar
1 tbsp. soy sauce
1/3 cup chopped green bell pepper

Directions:

1. In a large bowl, combine ground venison, cracker crumbs, onion, egg, milk, ginger and salt. Shape mixture by rounded tablespoonfuls into meatballs.
2. Heat olive oil in a large skillet over medium heat.
3. Place meatballs in skillet and cook until evenly brown, and meat is no longer pink.
4. Drain excess fat.
5. In a small bowl, combine the cornstarch, brown sugar, reserved pineapple juice, vinegar and soy sauce.
6. Mix until smooth, then pour into the skillet with meatballs.
7. Cook, stirring constantly, until mixture thickens and boils, about 5 minutes.
8. Stir in the green pepper and pineapple chunks.
9. Heat through and enjoy!

Mexican Venison Chili

Ingredients:

1/2 lb. ground pork sausage
2 lb. venison, cubed
2 med. onions, chopped
1 med. bell pepper, chopped
2 cloves garlic, minced
3 tbsp. chili powder or to desired taste
1 tbsp. salt
2 (15 oz.) cans kidney beans
1 qt. water
1/8 tsp. red pepper, if desired
1 tsp. paprika

Directions:

1. Brown pork sausage and venison in large saucepan on simmer.
2. Remove sausage and venison from saucepan.
3. Sauté onions and bell pepper.
4. Add sausage and venison; then add remaining ingredients and enough water to cover.
5. Simmer for 3-4 hours, stirring occasionally.
6. Add remaining water as needed.

Feta and Olive Venison Meatballs

Ingredients:

1 pound ground venison
1/2 cup chopped fresh parsley
2 tbsps. finely chopped onion
1/2 cup crumbled feta cheese
1/2 cup chopped green olives
2 eggs
1 tsp. Italian seasoning

Directions:

1. Preheat your oven's broiler.
2. In a large bowl, mix together ground venison with parsley, onion, feta cheese, green olives, eggs, and Italian seasoning.
3. Shape into 16 meatballs, and place 2 inches apart on a baking sheet.
4. Broil about 3 inches away from the heat until browned on top. Turn over, and broil on the other side.

Venison Stuffed Green Peppers

Ingredients:

6 green peppers
6 mushrooms, wipes & coarsely chopped
5 tsp. bacon drippings
1/8 tsp. pepper
2 1/2 cup diced left over cooked venison
2 scallions, washed and sliced thin
1 tsp. salt

Directions:

1. Wash green peppers, core and chop the cores.
2. Mix chopped ingredients.
3. Stuff peppers with the venison mixture.
4. Stand in shallow baking pan and bake in electric oven at 350 degrees for 45 minutes.

Venison Stroganoff

Ingredients:

1 pound venison, cut into cubes
Salt and pepper to taste
Garlic powder to taste
1 onion, chopped
2 (10.75 oz.) cans condensed cream of mushroom soup
1 (16 oz.) package uncooked egg noodles
1 (8 oz.) container sour cream

Directions:

1. Season venison with salt, pepper and garlic powder to taste.
2. Sauté onion in a large skillet; when soft, add venison and brown.
3. Drain when venison is no longer pink and add soup.
4. Reduce heat to low and simmer.
5. Meanwhile, bring a large pot of lightly salted water to a boil.
6. Add noodles and cook for 8 to 10 minutes or until al dente; drain.
7. When noodles are almost done cooking, stir sour cream into meat mixture.
8. Pour meat mixture over hot cooked noodles and serve.

Mustard Fried Venison

Ingredients:

3 to 4 lb. venison, cubed
1 med. jar prepared mustard
1 mustard jar full of red wine vinegar
Flour
Instant potato flakes

Directions:

1. Mix mustard and vinegar.
2. Add venison and marinate in refrigerator 12 to 24 hours.
3. Drain meat.
4. Mix equal parts of potato flakes and flour.
5. Coat meat with mixture then shake to remove excess.
6. Deep fry in hot oil.
7. Drain.

Venison Gyros

Ingredients:

2 tbsps. olive oil
1 1/2 tbsps. ground cumin
1 tbsp. minced garlic
2 tsps. dried marjoram
2 tsps. ground dried rosemary
1 tbsp. dried oregano
1 tbsp. red wine vinegar
Salt and pepper to taste
3 pounds venison, cut into 1/4 thick strips
1 (12 oz.) package pita breads, warmed

Directions:

1. Whisk together the olive oil, cumin, garlic, marjoram, rosemary, oregano, red wine vinegar, salt, and pepper in a large glass or ceramic bowl.
2. Add the venison strips, and toss to evenly coat.
3. Cover the bowl with plastic wrap, and marinate in the refrigerator at least 2 hours.
4. Heat a large skillet over medium-high heat.
5. Cook the venison strips, a half pound at a time, until the venison has browned on the outside and is no longer pink on the inside, about 8 minutes.
6. Pile the meat onto warmed pitas to serve.

Teriyaki Venison

Ingredients:

2 lbs. venison (round steak)
2 tbsp. vinegar
1/2 cup sugar
1/2 cup soy sauce
1 tsp. ginger
1 tsp. garlic, minced

Directions:

1. Rinse venison in cool water.
2. Then let meat "stand" for 20 minutes in cool water that 2 tbsps. of vinegar has been added.
3. Drain and rinse, drain and pat dry.
4. Cut meat into 1 1/2 x 1/2 inch strips.
5. Mix 1/2 cup sugar, 1/2 cup soy sauce, 1 tsp. vinegar, 1 tsp. ginger, 1 tsp. garlic in bowl.
6. Add venison strips. Let marinate for 20 minutes or longer.
7. Pour into 9 x 9 inch baking dish.
8. Cover.
9. Put in oven at 350 degrees for 30 minutes.
10. Serve over hot rice or noodles.

Venison & Wild Rice Casserole

Ingredients:

1 lb. ground venison
3 cup cooked wild rice
1 cup sliced celery
1 cup chopped onion
1 can cream of mushroom soup
1/2 lb. sliced fresh mushrooms
1 cup beef broth

Directions:

1. Brown venison in skillet.
2. Add celery, onion, broth and simmer until onions are tender.
3. Mix all ingredients.
4. Place in 3 quart casserole.
5. Cover and bake at 350 degrees for 1 hour.

Venison & Wild Rice Stew

Ingredients:

3 1/2 lbs. shoulder of venison, cut into 2 inch cubes
2 tsp. salt
1/8 tsp. pepper
2 qts. water
2 yellow onions
1 1/2 cup wild rice, washed in cold water

Directions:

1. Put the venison, onions and water in heavy kettle or Dutch oven and simmer covered, until venison is tender, approximately 3 hours.
2. Then add the wild rice, salt and pepper.
3. Cover and simmer for 20 to 25 minutes.
4. Stir the mixture and simmer about 20 minutes longer.
5. Leave uncovered. When the rice is tender and most of the liquid is absorbed, it is ready to enjoy.

Sweet And Sour Venison Stew

Ingredients:

2 lb. venison stew meat
1 lg. can tomatoes
1/2 cup brown sugar
1/2 cup vinegar
1 lg. onion, cut into pieces
1 lg. green pepper, cut into pieces

Directions:

1. Brown venison stew meat in oil in large Dutch oven.
2. Add onion and cook lightly.
3. Add mashed tomatoes, vinegar, and brown sugar.
4. Put in enough water so it won't stick.
5. Cook several hours until tender. The last 10 minutes of cooking, add green pepper strips.

Cajun Venison

Ingredients:

2 tbsp. cajun seasoning
8 thin 1/8" sliced venison
2 tbsp. butter
1 tbsp. currant jelly
1/4 cup dry white wine

Directions:

1. Rub Cajun seasoning into venison.
2. In a heavy pan heat butter.
3. Add venison and cook for 1 minute.
4. Turn slices and cook for another minute.
5. Add currant jelly and white wine and allow to simmer for 5 minutes.
6. Serve on a warm platter. Yield 4 servings.

Venison Goulash

Ingredients:

2 lbs. sm. white onions, sliced
8 oz. fat (lard or canned vegetable shortening)
3 lbs. stewing venison, cubed
1 tbsp. butter
1 1/2 tbsp. paprika
2 cans beef broth
Egg noodles for serving.

Directions:

1. Fry onions in fat until soft.
2. Add cubed venison and brown on all sides.
3. Sprinkle butter and paprika over meat and cover with beef broth.
4. Cover pot and simmer slowly 3 hours or until meat is tender, stirring often and from time to time adding more warm beef broth.
5. Gravy should be sort of thick.
6. Cook noodles according to package directions.
7. Serve meat and gravy over the noodles and enjoy!

Venison Hash

Ingredients:

2 cup diced venison, boiled
3 tbsp. bacon drippings
1 lg. onion, diced
2 or 3 lg. potatoes, diced
Salt and pepper to taste
1/2 to 1 cup water

Directions:

1. Use a heavy skillet and heat bacon drippings.
2. Add onions and sauté until tender.
3. Add venison, potatoes, salt and pepper.
4. Cook over moderate heat until the mixture begins to brown.
5. Reduce heat and add water.
6. Simmer about 5-10 minutes.
7. Serve and enjoy!

Venison Cider Stew

Ingredients:

2 tbsp. venison, cubed
1 tsp. dried onion flakes
2 tsp. salt
1/4 tsp. thyme
1/4 tsp. nutmeg
3 potatoes, cut into chunks
4 carrots, cut into chunks
1 apple, chopped
1 cup tart apple cider

Directions:

1. Brown the venison in a skillet, sprinkling on the onion, salt, thyme and nutmeg while stirring continually.
2. Transfer the seasoned meat to a crock pot or stew pot.
3. Add the vegetables and apple, then pour cider over the top.
4. Slow cook on very low heat for at least 3 hours
5. If too much liquid begins to evaporate, add mixture of 1/2 water with 1/2 cup cider.
6. Serve and enjoy!

Venison Fingers

Ingredients:

1 lb. venison steak
1 cup milk
1 cup all-purpose flour
2 eggs, slightly beaten
1 stack soda crackers, crushed

Directions:

1. Cut venison into 1/2 inch strips about 1 inch long.
2. Soak in milk for 5 minutes.
3. Dip in flour, then egg and then crackers.
4. Fry for about 5 minutes or until golden brown.

Venison Cream Cheese Casserole

Ingredients:

1 1/2 lbs. ground venison, season well to taste
1 onion, chopped
1 green pepper, chopped
16 oz. fresh mushrooms, sliced
2 tbsp. minced garlic
12 oz. creamed cottage cheese
16 oz. cream cheese, softened
8 oz. sour cream
1 (32 oz.) jar spaghetti sauce
2 tsp. fennel seed
3/4 bag of egg noodles, cooked & drained
2 cup shredded cheddar or Colby cheese

Directions:

1. Brown venison with onion and minced garlic.
2. Add butter to venison if needed.
3. Add green pepper, fresh mushrooms, fennel seed and spaghetti sauce.
4. While this mixture simmers for 10 minutes, cook egg noodle and drain and rinse. In medium bowl cream together cottage cheese, cream cheese and sour cream.
5. Spray a 9 x 13 inch pan with cooking spray and layer with noodles, cheese mixture and spaghetti sauce.
6. Top with shredded cheese and bake for 1 hour at 325 degrees.
7. Cover with foil if edges of casserole seem to darken.

Venison Jerky

Ingredients:

4 1/2 tsp. pickling salt
1 1/2 tsp. garlic powder
1 1/2 tsp. pepper
1-2 lb. venison

Directions:

1. Hickory chips for smoker or 2 tbsp. liquid smoke for oven method
2. Mix salt, garlic powder, and pepper in a bowl.
3. Slice venison into strips about 1/8 inch thick.
4. Place strips on cutting board side by side and sprinkle half the mixture over meat.
5. Pound meat lightly.
6. Turn meat over and repeat. Hang in smoker for about 5 hours.
7. If you don't have a smoker, mix venison with liquid smoke in a bowl first, then follow the smoker recipe.
8. Hang strips on oven rack set on "warm" with door slightly ajar for 5-6 hours.

Tabasco Venison Jerky

Ingredients:

20 lbs. stripped venison
1 sm. bottle Tabasco sauce
4 (5 oz.) bottles Worcestershire sauce
2 (6 oz.) bottles soy sauce
1 box red pepper
1 sm. bottle onion salt
1 bottle liquid hickory smoke (omit if using smoker)

Directions:

1. Mix all ingredients and pour over venison as a marinade.
2. Allow to stand overnight.
3. Place venison strips on cookie sheet or foil in a 175 degree oven.
4. Bake for approximately 2 hours, or until dry.
5. Be sure to leave door of oven open a crack.
6. Prep. time: 12 hours.

Venison Pizzas

Ingredients:

1 lb. ground venison or venison sausage
1 can pizza sauce
Sliced mushrooms, olives, or sliced fresh onions
Salt and pepper to taste
1 can biscuits
Grated cheese, sharp or Mozzarella

Directions:

1. Cook venison or sausage in a skillet and drain.
2. Slices of link sausage may be used.
3. Season meat to taste if needed.
4. Roll out canned biscuits in small pizza rounds.
5. Place on a cookie or pizza sheet. spread with 1 tbsp. of pizza sauce, add venison and garnish.
6. Broil in the oven after topping with cheese, about 10-15 minutes.

Venison Sauerbraten

Ingredients:

3 to 3 1/2 lb. venison chuck roast
12 peppercorns
6 whole cloves
1 1/2 cup red wine vinegar
2 tbsp. shortening
2 tbsp. sugar
2 onions, sliced
2 bay leaves
12 juniper berries, if desired
2 tbsp. salt
1 cup boiling water
12 gingersnaps, crushed (about 3/4 c.)

Directions:

1. Place roast in an earthenware bowl or glass baking dish with onions, bay leaves, peppercorns, berries, cloves, salt, vinegar, and boiling water.
2. Cover bowl with plastic wrap. Marinate 3 days or longer in refrigerator, turning meat twice a day with 2 wooden spoons.
3. Drain meat, reserving marinade. Brown meat on all sides in hot shortening in a heavy skillet.
4. Add marinade mixture.
5. Cover skillet and simmer.
6. Add water if necessary to measure 2 1/2 cups of liquid.
7. Pour liquid into skillet.
8. Cover and simmer 10 minutes, stir gingersnaps and sugar into liquid.
9. Cover and simmer gently 3 minutes.
10. Serve meat and onions on a platter. Accompany with gingersnap gravy.
1. o make the tops of the pies, roll out each smaller piece of dough to about the same thickness -- they should be smaller, about 5 inches in diameter. Lay the top on the venison filling.
2. Now take up the bottom of the larger piece of dough and attach it to the top piece of dough by pinching and crimping it over.
3. Do this all around the pie to seal it. With a very sharp knife slice vents in the top of the pie.
4. Beat the egg with a little water and paint all the pies with it.
5. Bake in the oven for 25 to 35 minutes, or until they are golden brown. Let the pies rest on a rack for at least 10 minutes before eating. They are good hot, cold or at room temperature.

Venison Vegetable Pot Pie

Ingredients:

Venison neck or backbone, broken into chunks
1 qt. water
1 rib celery, chopped
2 tsp. salt
1/2 tsp. black pepper
1 beef bouillon cube
1 cup all-purpose flour
1/2 tsp. salt
1/2 cup vegetable shortening
4 tbsp. ice water
2 carrots, cooked & diced
1/2 cup canned corn
1/2 cup melted butter
1/4 cup all-purpose flour
2 cup venison broth
1/2 cup milk

Directions:

1. Place venison, water, celery, salt, pepper and bouillon cube in a pot; cover and boil.
2. Reduce heat and simmer for 2 hours.
3. Remove bones from pot; let cool; pick meat and dice. Strain broth and set aside.
4. Sift 1 cup flour with 1/2 tsp. salt in a bowl; add shortening and work with hands until flour and shortening have blended.
5. Add water and mix quickly.
6. Place dough on a plate; cover with wax paper and refrigerate 15 minutes.
7. Then roll out dough to make a top crust for the pie.
8. When finished with dough, melt 1/2 cup butter in saucepan, add 1/4 cup flour and stir until paste becomes almond colored.
9. Stir in venison broth and add milk after sauce thickens.
10. Add vegetables, folding in gently, and place in a casserole dish.
11. Cover with pastry crust.
12. Brush with melted butter and bake at 425 degrees until crust has browned lightly.

Venison Shepherd's Pie

Ingredients:

4 large potatoes, peeled and cubed
Salt and pepper to taste
2 tbsps. butter
1/2 cup half-and-half cream
1/2 pound ground venison
1/4 tsp. Italian seasoning
1 small onion, chopped
1 parsnip, peeled and diced
2 cups frozen mixed vegetables
1 tbsp. butter, melted
1/4 tsp. garlic powder

Directions:

1. Place potatoes into a large pot and cover with salted water.
2. Bring to a boil, then reduce heat to medium-low, cover, and simmer until tender, about 20 minutes.
3. Drain and allow to steam dry for a minute or two, then mash with salt, pepper, 2 tbsps. butter, and half-and-half; set aside.
4. Preheat oven to 400 degrees F (200 degrees C).
5. Meanwhile, stir together the elk meat, Italian seasoning, salt, and pepper in a skillet over medium-high heat until crumbly and no longer pink, about 5 minutes.
6. Spread the cooked elk meat into a 9-inch pie plate or baking dish and return the skillet to the stove over medium heat.
7. Place the onion, parsnip, and garlic powder in the skillet, season to taste with salt and pepper, and cook until the turnip has softened, about 10 minutes.
8. Stir in the mixed vegetables and cook an additional 5 minutes, then spread in the pie plate over the elk.
9. Finally, spread the mashed potatoes evenly over the top, and brush the melted butter on the potatoes.
10. Bake in preheated oven until the potatoes begin to turn golden brown, about 30 minutes.
11. Serve hot.

Venison Swedish Meatballs

Meatball Ingredients:

1 1/2 lbs. ground venison
tsp. ground parsley
1 1/2 cup seasoned bread crumbs
2 eggs
1/2 tsp. garlic powder
1/2 tsp. onion powder

Sauce Ingredients:

8 oz. tomatoes
1 can jellied cranberry sauce

Directions:

1. Mix all the meatball ingredients together.
2. Roll into balls 1 inch in diameter.
3. Brown meatballs in pan, then remove and drain.
4. Prepare the sauce by dissolving the cranberry sauce in the tomatoes.
5. When the mixture is hot, add the meatballs and simmer on low heat for 20 minutes.
6. Place in crock pot for warming and serving.

Venison Summer Sausage

Ingredients:

2 lb. venison hamburger
2 tbsp. Morton Tender Quick Salt
1/2 tsp. mustard seed
1/2 tsp. marjoram
1/4 tsp. sage
1 tsp. sugar
1 cup cold water
1 tsp. ground black pepper
1 tsp. crushed red pepper
1/2 tsp. garlic powder

Directions:

1. Combine and mix water and seasonings.
2. Pour over venison hamburger and mix thoroughly.
3. Form in rolls on foil.
4. Wrap tight and twist ends.
5. Boil in foil for 1 hour.
6. Split bottom of foil and drain juices on rack. Cool.
7. Serve and enjoy!

Venison Zucchini Lasagna

Ingredients:

1/2 lb. ground venison
1 cup onion, chopped
1 (15 oz.) can tomato sauce
1/2 tsp. salt
1/2 tsp. oregano
1/4 tsp. basil
1/8 tsp. pepper
4 med. zucchini, cut into 1/4 inch slices
1 container low-fat cottage cheese (sm. curd)
1 egg
2 tbsp. flour
1/4 lb. skim milk Mozzarella, shredded

Directions:

1. Brown venison and onion.
2. Drain.
3. Add tomato sauce, seasonings, and 1 tbsp. flour.
4. Combine cottage cheese with the egg.
5. Arrange zucchini in 12 x 8 inch pan in single layer.
6. Sprinkle with remaining tbsp. flour.
7. Put layer of cottage cheese mixture over zucchini, then a Mozzarella cheese layer; repeat, ending with meat mixture.
8. Bake at 350 degrees for 40 minutes.
9. Let stand 15 minutes before cutting.

Venison-Stuffed Cabbage Leaves

Ingredients:

2 lbs. ground venison
3 tbsp. butter
1 tbsp. chopped dill
12 cabbage leaves
5 tbsp. chopped onion
2 cup cooked rice
Salt and pepper to taste
1 (8 oz.) can tomato sauce

Directions:

1. Brown venison and onion in butter; mix in rice, dill, salt, and pepper.
2. Place cabbage leaves in boiling water for 1 minute; drain, dry on paper towels.
3. Place equal amount of meat mixture in center of each leaf.
4. Fold leaf over, secure with toothpicks.
5. Place filled leaves in greased baking dish; pour tomato sauce over leaves.
6. Bake at 325 degrees for about 45 minutes.

Broccoli Venison Casserole

Ingredients:

1 lb. fresh broccoli or 16 oz. pkg. frozen broccoli
1 tbsp. butter
1/2 tsp. salt
1 cup chopped cooked venison
2 hard cooked eggs, chopped
2 tbsp. finely chopped onion
1/2 cup cracker crumbs
1 tbsp. flour
1 cup milk
1/2 cup grated sharp cheese
1 tbsp. lemon juice
2 tsp. parsley flakes

Directions:

1. Preheat oven to 325 degrees.
2. Cook broccoli until just barely tender.
3. Drain.
4. Make a white sauce by melting butter, adding flour and salt and cooking 1 minute.
5. Remove from heat and add milk.
6. Return to fire and cook until sauce bubbles, stirring constantly.

Venison Chili Con Carne

Ingredients:

1/2 lb. dried kidney beans
1/4 lb. beef suet
3 sliced cloves of garlic
Chili powder
Salt
1 qt. water
1 sliced onion
1 lb. lean ground venison
Paprika

Directions:

1. Soak the dried kidney beans according to the directions on the package.
2. Cook in the same soaking water, adding more if needed.
3. Cut the suet into small pieces.
4. Fry until crisp.
5. Add the meat and brown, add the onion and garlic and brown for an additional 3 minutes.

Chicken Fried Venison, Steak

Ingredients:

1 1/2 lb. venison steak, 1/2 inch thick
1 tbsp. milk
1 beaten egg
1 cup fine cracker crumbs
1/4 cup salad oil
Salt and pepper

Directions:

1. Pound steak thoroughly, cut into serving pieces.
2. Combine milk and beaten egg.
3. Dip meat into egg then in crumbs.
4. Slowly brown meat, cover, cook over low heat, 35 to 45 minutes or until meat is tender.
5. Continue roasting, uncovered, until bread crumbs are brown.

Burgundy Venison

Ingredients:

2 lbs. venison, cut up like stew meat
1/2 cup Burgundy wine
1 sm. can mushrooms
1 can cream of mushroom soup
1 pkg. dry onion soup mix

Directions:

1. Put everything in a slow cooker.
2. Mix until well blended.
3. Cook all day.
4. Serve and enjoy!

Cranberry Venison Stew

Ingredients:

3 lbs. venison or chuck, cut into 1 inch cubes
1/4 cup butter
2 lg. onion, chopped
2 cup cranberries
3 (10 1/2 oz.) cans condensed beef broth
2 cloves garlic
Salt & pepper
2 cup celery, cut in 1 inch pieces
6 potatoes, peeled and halved
6 carrots, cut in 1 inch pieces
1 (12 oz.) can corn, drained
1/4 cup flour mixed with 1/3 cup water

Directions:

1. In a large Dutch oven brown beef on all sides in butter.
2. Add onions and cranberries.
3. Cook 5 minutes or until onions are tender.
4. Stir in broth and garlic.
5. Cover and simmer for 1 1/2 hours or until meat is tender.
6. Stir in celery, potatoes, carrots and corn.
7. Simmer 20 minutes longer or until vegetables are fork tender.
8. Stir in flour mixture.
9. Cook until gravy is thickened.
10. Season to taste with salt.

Venison Breakfast Sausage

Ingredients:

1 pound ground venison
8 oz. bacon, minced
1 tsp. ground sage
1/2 tsp. ground ginger
1/4 tsp. pepper
3/4 tsp. onion salt

Directions:

1. Combine the venison, bacon, sage, ginger, pepper, and onion salt in a large bowl; mix well.
2. Shape into 12 patties using about 1/4 cup of mixture per patty.
3. Patties can either be pan-fried or frozen for later use.

Bacon-Wrapped Venison Tenderloin

Ingredients:

6 thick slices bacon
2 (3/4 pound) venison tenderloin roasts
2 tsps. olive oil, divided
1/4 tsp. onion powder, divided
Kosher salt and ground black pepper to taste
2 tbsps. butter

Directions:

1. Preheat oven to 375 degrees F (190 degrees C).
2. Place bacon on a slotted baking pan.
3. Bake bacon in the preheated oven until partially cooked but still flexible, 6 to 8 minutes.
4. Brush venison tenderloins with olive oil and season with onion powder, salt, and black pepper.
5. Place tenderloin roasts side by side and wrap them together in strips of partially cooked bacon.
6. Place into a roasting pan.
7. Roast until bacon is browned and an instant-read meat thermometer inserted into the thickest part of a tenderloin reads at least 145 degrees F (65 degrees C), about 1 hour.
8. Heat butter in a saucepan over medium heat.
9. Cook and stir mushrooms and garlic in hot butter until mushrooms are soft, 8 to 10 minutes.
10. Stir green onion into mushroom mixture; pour in cream.
11. Cook, stirring often, until sauce is heated through.
12. Serve sauce with tenderloins.

Venison Pot Roast and Gravy

Ingredients:

1 pound boneless venison roast, thinly sliced across the grain
1 tbsp. minced garlic
1 tbsp. grill seasoning
1 tsp. chili powder
2 cups beef broth
1/4 cup butter
1/4 cup flour

Directions:

1. Preheat oven to 350 degrees F (175 degrees C).
2. Season the venison with garlic, grill seasoning, and chili powder.
3. Place into a casserole dish, and pour in the beef broth.
4. Cover the dish with a lid, and bake in preheated oven until the venison is tender, about 1 hour.
5. Meanwhile, melt the butter in a saucepan over medium heat. Once the butter begins to bubble, whisk in the flour.
6. Cook while whisking constantly until the flour turns a golden yellow, and the bubbling slows, about 10 minutes.
7. When the venison has finished cooking, whisk 1 1/2 cups of the broth from the venison roast into the flour roux, and simmer for 15 minutes, whisking frequently.
8. Add the venison to the gravy and serve.

Venison-Bacon White Chili

Ingredients:

6 tbsps. butter
2 tbsps. all-purpose flour
1/2 tsp. ground white pepper
4 tsps. salt, divided
2 tbsps. brown sugar
1 tsp. ground cinnamon
1/2 tsp. ground nutmeg
4 cups chicken broth
1 (4 oz.) can green chiles, diced, liquid reserved
6 cloves garlic, crushed
2 tsps. chili powder, divided
2 tsps. cayenne pepper, divided
1 tbsp. ground cumin
1 tbsp. dried cilantro
1 tsp. ground coriander seed
1 tsp. dried oregano
1 (15 oz.) can whole kernel corn, drained
1 (15 oz.) can great northern beans, rinsed and drained
1 pound ground venison
1 pound sliced bacon, diced
1 red onion, chopped6 cloves garlic, minced

Directions:

1. Melt the butter in a large pot over medium-low heat.
2. Stir in flour until smooth.
3. Cook and stir until the flour turns dark, about 15 to 20 minutes.
4. Stir in the white pepper, 1 tsp. of salt, brown sugar, cinnamon and nutmeg until smooth.
5. Gradually whisk in the chicken broth so that no lumps form.
6. Add the green chilies with their liquid, and the crushed garlic cloves.
7. Season with 1 tsp. of chili powder, 1 tsp. of cayenne, cumin, cilantro, coriander and oregano.
8. Stir in the corn and beans, and bring to a simmer.
9. Place the bacon in a large skillet over medium-high heat.
10. Cook, turning occasionally until browned.
11. Add the onion and minced garlic; cook and stir for a few minutes.
12. Add the venison, and season with remaining 3 tsps. of salt, 1 tsp. of chili powder and 1 tsp. of cayenne pepper.
13. Cook, stirring to break the venison to your desired texture, until evenly browned.
14. Transfer the meat mixture to the pot, and simmer over low heat for at least 1 hour, stirring occasionally.

Mexican Venison Skillet

Ingredients:

2 tbsps. butter or margarine
1 pound ground venison
2 tsps. minced garlic
1 onion, chopped
2 tbsps. butter or margarine
1 (7 oz.) box Spanish rice mix
3 cups water
1 (14.5 oz.) can stewed tomatoes, cut up
1/2 cup salsa
1 (15.5 oz.) can kidney beans, rinsed and drained
1 (15.5 oz.) can sweet corn, drained

Directions:

1. Melt butter in a large skillet over medium-high heat.
2. Add venison and cook until no longer pink, stirring to break up.
3. Stir in garlic and onion, and continue cooking until the onion has softened and turned translucent, about 2 minutes.
4. Meanwhile, melt remaining 2 tbsps. butter in a saucepan over medium heat.
5. Stir in Spanish rice mix, and cook until lightly golden, about 5 minutes.
6. Stir in cooked venison, water, tomatoes, salsa, and kidney beans; bring to a boil, then reduce heat to medium-low and simmer for 15 minutes.
7. Stir in corn, and continue cooking until the rice is tender, about 5 minutes.

Fried Venison Backstrap

Ingredients:

1 (2 pound) venison backstrap, cut into 1/4 inch thick slices
2 cups milk
2 tbsps. hot pepper sauce
2 eggs
1/2 cup milk
3 cups all-purpose flour
2 tbsps. salt
1 tbsp. ground black pepper
3 cups vegetable oil for frying

Directions:

1. Place the venison slices into a shallow bowl and pour in the milk and hot sauce.
2. Stir to coat, then cover and marinate for 1 hour.
3. Heat the vegetable oil in an electric skillet to 325 degrees F (165 degrees C).
4. In a shallow bowl, whisk together the eggs and milk.
5. In a separate bowl, stir together the flour, salt and pepper.
6. Dip the venison slices into the flour, then into the egg and milk, then back into the flour. Shake off excess flour.
7. Fry in the hot oil until lightly browned on each side, about 3 minutes.
8. Remove with tongs and drain briefly on paper towels before serving.

Baked Spaghetti with Venison

Ingredients:

1 (8 oz.) package angel hair pasta
2 tbsps. olive oil
1 pound cubed lean venison
1 small onion, diced
1 bell pepper, diced
1 (6 oz.) can tomato paste
2 (15 oz.) cans tomato sauce
1 tsp. garlic salt
1 1/2 tsps. dried dill
1 1/2 tsps. dried marjoram
1 1/2 tsps. Italian seasoning
4 oz. shredded Mozzarella cheese
1/4 cup grated Parmesan cheese

Directions:

1. Preheat oven to 350 degrees F (175 degrees C). Spray a casserole dish with cooking spray.
2. Bring a large pot of lightly salted water to a boil.
3. Add spaghetti and cook for 3 to 5 minutes or until al dente; drain.
4. Meanwhile, heat olive oil in a large skillet over medium-high heat until it begins to smoke.
5. Add venison and cook until well browned, about 5 minutes.
6. Stir in onion and green pepper, continue cooking until softened, about 4 minutes.
7. Add tomato paste and tomato sauce, season with garlic salt, dill, marjoram, and Italian seasoning.
8. Bring to a boil, then reduce heat to medium, and simmer for 5 minutes.
9. Place drained pasta into prepared casserole dish and pour venison overtop. sprinkle with Mozzarella and Parmesan cheeses.
10. Bake in preheated oven until the cheese is bubbly and browned, about 25 minutes.

Venison Wellington

Ingredients:

2 tbsps. butter, divided, or as needed
1 venison backstrap, cut in half
1 (10 oz.) package sliced fresh mushrooms
1 medium onion, diced
2 cloves garlic, diced
1/2 tbsp. Worcestershire sauce
1 tbsp. ground thyme, or to taste
salt and ground black pepper to taste
1 pound bacon, or as needed
1 (17.5 oz.) package frozen puff pastry, thawed
1 egg yolk
1 tbsp. water, or as needed

Directions:

1. Preheat the oven to 450 degrees F (230 degrees C).
2. Melt 1 tbsp. butter in a hot pan over medium-high heat. Brown venison in the hot butter, about 2 minutes per side.
3. Set meat aside.
4. Melt remaining butter in the pan over medium-high heat.
5. Add mushrooms, onion, garlic, and Worcestershire sauce. Sauté until mushrooms are soft, 5 to 7 minutes.
6. Set aside and allow to cool.
7. Spread thyme, salt, and pepper onto a large cutting board and roll backstrap halves on top to form a coating of herbs.
8. Wrap each piece of backstrap in enough bacon to cover it.
9. Unfold 1 puff pastry and place first piece of backstrap into the center.
10. Bring the sides of the pastry together and pinch to seal.
11. Repeat with other backstrap and remaining pastry.
12. Place each into an ungreased baking dish.
13. Mix egg yolk and water together in a small bowl. Coat the tops of the dough.
14. Bake in the preheated oven for 10 minutes.
15. Reduce heat to 425 degrees F (220 degrees C). Continue to bake until dough is golden brown, 10 to 15 minutes more.

Texas Venison

Ingredients:

2 pounds venison steaks
1 1/2 tsps. seasoned salt, divided (see Note)
1 cup all-purpose flour
4 tbsps. vegetable oil
1/2 tsp. ground cumin
1/2 cup onion, halved and sliced
2 beef bouillon cubes
1/2 tsp. dried Mexican oregano
1 bay leaf
2 dried red chile peppers
2 cups water

Directions:

1. Lightly season the venison steaks with 1/2 tsp. of Papa's Seasoning Salt (see below).
2. Cut the steaks into bite-sized pieces.
3. Mix the flour with 1 tsp. of Papa's salt; reserve 1 tbsp. of the flour mixture and set aside.
4. Toss the cubed meat in the seasoned flour.
5. Heat the oil in the pressure cooker or a skillet over medium-high heat.
6. Add the meat cubes in batches and cook until richly browned on all sides.
7. Remove the meat and set aside.
8. Reduce the heat to medium, and stir the reserved tbsp. of seasoned flour and the ground cumin into the pan drippings.
9. Cook and stir until the flour has lost its raw smell and is lightly browned, about 5 minutes.
10. Add the sliced onion and cook, stirring often, until the onion has softened, about 5 minutes.
11. Return the meat to the pan, along with the beef bouillon cubes, Mexican oregano, bay leaf, and chile peppers (remove the stems, but leave them whole).
12. Pour in the water and seal the pressure cooker, turning the heat up to high.
13. Bring the pressure up to high and reduce the heat to maintain the pressure.
14. Cook at high pressure for 15 minutes. Turn off the heat and let the pressure drop naturally.
15. Remove the lid.

16. Remove the chile peppers and bay leaf; squeeze the pulp from the peppers, returning the pulp to the pan and discarding the skins and the bay leaf. Taste and adjust the seasonings.

Venison Pastrami

Ingredients:

5 tbsps. sugar-based curing mixture (such as Morton® Quick Cure®)
2 tbsps. brown sugar, or as needed
1 tbsp. coarsely ground black pepper, or as needed
1 tbsp. paprika
1 tbsp. crushed bay leaf
1 tsp. ground allspice
1/2 tsp. garlic powder
5 pounds venison rump roast

Directions:

1. Whisk together curing mixture, brown sugar, pepper, paprika, bay leaf, allspice, and garlic powder in a bowl. Rub mixture over venison roast, and wrap tightly in plastic wrap.
2. Place roast in a bowl; refrigerate for 5 days.
3. Remove roast from the refrigerator and rinse thoroughly to remove the curing mixture.
4. Place in a bowl with water to cover, and soak, refrigerated, for 2 hours.
5. Drain.
6. Preheat oven to 250 degrees F (120 degrees C).
7. Season roast with additional black pepper and brown sugar, and place in a roasting pan.
8. Bake, uncovered, in the preheated oven until a meat thermometer inserted near the center reads 160 degrees F (70 degrees C), about 2 hours.

Corned Venison

Ingredients:

2 cups water
6 tbsps. sugar-based curing mixture (such as Morton® Tender Quick®)
1/2 cup brown sugar
4 1/2 tsps. pickling spice
1 tbsp. garlic powder
6 cups cold water
5 pounds boneless shoulder venison roast

Directions:

1. Bring 2 cups of water to a boil in a saucepan over high heat.
2. Stir in the curing mixture, brown sugar, pickling spice, and garlic powder; stir until dissolved then remove from the heat.
3. Pour 6 cups of cold water into a 2-gallon container, and stir in the spice mixture.
4. Place the boneless venison into the brine, cover and refrigerate.
5. Leave the venison in the refrigerator to brine for 5 days, turning the meat over every day.
6. To cook, rinse the meat well, place into a large pot, and cover with water.
7. Bring to a boil, then reduce heat to medium-low, cover, and simmer for 4 hours.
8. Remove the venison from the pot, and allow to rest for 30 minutes before slicing.

Venison with Blackberry Wine Sauce

Ingredients:

2 tbsps. shallot, minced
1 tsp. minced garlic
3 tbsps. blackberry jam
1 cup red wine
1 cup beef stock
1 tbsp. butter
salt and ground black pepper to taste
4 (1/2 pound) venison steaks
12 fresh blackberries

Directions:

1. Heat shallots, garlic, blackberry jam, and red wine in a saucepan over medium-high heat. Simmer until reduced to 1/2 cup of liquid, about 15 minutes.
2. Strain liquid through a fine mesh sieve and set aside.
3. Heat the beef broth in a separate skillet over medium-high heat until reduced by half, 15 to 20 minutes.
4. Whisk the two reduced sauces together, and stir in the butter.
5. Season with salt and pepper.
6. Heat a skillet over medium-high heat.
7. Cook the venison steaks until they are beginning to firm, and are hot and slightly pink in the center, 3 to 4 minutes per side.
8. An instant-read thermometer inserted into the center should read at least 145 degrees F (65 degrees C).
9. Serve the steaks with the sauce and a few fresh blackberries.

Venison Tequila Chili

Ingredients:

2 tbsps. vegetable oil
3 pounds ground venison
2 stalks celery, diced
3 cups chopped white onion
1/2 tsp. dried red pepper flakes
1 tbsp. garlic powder
1/4 cup chili powder
2 (28 oz.) cans diced tomatoes
1 (16 oz.) can tomato sauce
1/2 cup gold tequila
1/2 cup orange juice
2 (15 oz.) cans chili beans in sauce

Directions:

1. Heat the oil in a large pot over medium-high heat.
2. Add the ground venison and cook, stirring to crumble, until no longer pink.
3. Mix in the celery and onion; cook and stir until tender.
4. Season with red pepper flakes, garlic powder and chili powder.
5. Cook and stir for a minute to intensify the flavors.
6. Pour in the tomatoes, tomato sauce, tequila and orange juice; simmer over low heat, uncovered, for 2 hours. After 2 hours, mix the beans into the chili and simmer for another 30 minutes.

Venison Pasta Casserole

Ingredients:

1 (16 oz.) package medium tube pasta
1 tbsp. olive oil
1 yellow onion, chopped
1 pound ground venison
1 (15 oz.) can tomato sauce
1/4 tsp. dried basil
? tsp. garlic powder
salt and pepper to taste
1/4 cup grated Parmesan cheese
3 cups grated Mozzarella cheese

Directions:

1. Preheat oven to 375 degrees F (190 degrees C).
2. Lightly grease a 9x13 inch baking dish.
3. Bring a large pot of lightly salted water to a boil.
4. Add the pasta and cook until al dente, about 8 to 10 minutes.
5. Drain and reserve pasta.
6. Meanwhile, place the olive oil into a skillet set over medium-high heat.
7. Stir in the onion, and cook until soft and translucent, about 5 minutes.
8. Add the venison and cook until crumbled and no longer pink, about 10 minutes.
9. Drain, if necessary.
10. Stir in the tomato sauce, basil, and garlic powder.
11. Season to taste with salt and pepper, and turn off the heat.
12. Assemble the casserole by spooning a layer of the venison sauce over the bottom of the prepared baking dish.
13. Sprinkle the sauce with Parmesan cheese, and layer with cooked pasta.
14. Top with the sauce, layer with pasta, and half of the Mozzarella.
15. Repeat the layers to use the remaining ingredients, ending with a layer of Mozzarella cheese.
16. Cover the dish with aluminum foil.
17. Bake in preheated oven for 20 minutes.
18. Remove the foil cover and bake until the cheese topping is light gold, about 10 minutes more.

Spicy Venison Meatballs

Ingredients:

1 pound ground venison
4 oz. bulk hot Italian sausage
3/4 cup panko bread crumbs
2 eggs
1 tsp. salt
1 tsp. Italian seasoning
1 tsp. crushed red pepper
1/2 tsp. garlic powder

Directions:

1. Preheat the oven to 400 degrees F (200 degrees C). Line a baking sheet with aluminum foil and place a cooling rack on top.
2. Combine ground venison, Italian sausage, bread crumbs, eggs, salt, Italian seasoning, red pepper, and garlic powder in a large bowl and mix until well combined. Scoop meat from the bowl and form into 1 1/2-inch balls.
3. Place meatballs on top of the cooling rack.
4. Bake in the preheated oven until cooked though, about 20 minutes. An instant-read thermometer inserted into the center should read at least 160 degrees F (70 degrees C).
5. Remove from oven and let rest for 5 minutes before serving.

Texas Venison Corn Chowder

Ingredients:

1/4 cup butter
1 green bell pepper, chopped
? cup chopped onion
3 cups whole milk
1 (10.75 oz.) can condensed cream of potato soup
1 tbsp. Worcestershire sauce
1 pound ground venison
1 (16 oz.) can cream-style corn
ground black pepper to taste
4 cups shredded Cheddar cheese

Directions:

1. Melt butter in a large pot over medium-high heat. Sauté green bell pepper and onion until tender, 5 to 10 minutes.
2. Stir in milk, potato soup, and Worcestershire sauce. Let soup simmer, uncovered, for 15 minutes.
3. Heat a large skillet over medium-high heat.
4. Add venison; cook and stir until browned and crumbly, 5 to 7 minutes.
5. Drain and discard grease.
6. Add venison to the soup; stir in corn.
7. Season with pepper. Simmer until flavors meld, at least 15 minutes.
8. Stir in cheese until melted.

Cheddar Venison Stuffed Peppers

Ingredients:

4 tsps. unsalted butter
1 onion, chopped
1 1/2 pounds ground venison
1 1/2 cups shredded Cheddar cheese, divided
1 (6 oz.) box sage stuffing mix
1 tsp. garlic powder
1/2 tsp. ground black pepper
1/4 tsp. salt
1 cup heavy whipping cream, or as needed
4 large green bell peppers, halved, stems and seeds removed

Directions:

1. Heat butter in a skillet over medium heat.
2. Add onion and cook until softened, 3 to 5 minutes.
3. Combine venison, 1/2 the Cheddar cheese, stuffing mix, garlic powder, black pepper, and salt in a bowl.
4. Mix until well blended.
5. Add enough cream to create a thick, doughy texture.
6. Add cooked onions and mix to blend.
7. Preheat the oven to 350 degrees F (175 degrees C).
8. Grease a glass baking dish.
9. Arrange bell pepper halves in the prepared baking dish, cut-sides up.
10. Form meat mixture into 8 meatballs using your hands.
11. Stuff meatballs into bell pepper halves in the baking dish.
12. Bake in the preheated oven for 60 minutes.
13. Top with remaining Cheddar cheese and continue baking until melted and starting to brown, about 15 minutes more.

About the Author

Laura Sommers is **The Recipe Lady!**

She lives on a small farm in Baltimore County, Maryland and has a passion for all things domestic especially when it comes to saving money. She has a profitable eBay business and is a couponing addict. Follow her tips and tricks to learn how to make delicious meals on a budget, save money or to learn the latest life hack!

Follow her on Pinterest:

http://pinterest.com/therecipelady1

Visit the Recipe Lady's blog for even more great recipes:

http://the-recipe-lady.blogspot.com/

Visit her Amazon Author Page to see her latest books:

amazon.com/author/laurasommers

Follow the Recipe Lady on Facebook:

https://www.facebook.com/therecipegirl

Follow her on Twitter:

https://twitter.com/TheRecipeLady1

Other Books by Laura Sommers

German Christmas Cookbook

Christmas Hot Chocolate Recipes

Christmas Fruitcake Recipes

Christmas Cookies

Christmas Pie Cookbook

Christmas Eggnog Cookbook

Christmas Coffee Cookbook

Christmas Candy Cane Cookbook

Christmas Gingerbread Recipes

Christmas Stuffing Recipes

Made in the USA
Coppell, TX
29 November 2023